WHISPERS OF HOPE

Waiting for Rain in Drought Ravaged Australia

Featuring the Poetry and Photography of

Tammy Harrison

Copyright © 2020 by Tammy Harrison

All rights reserved.

This book or any portion thereof

may not be reproduced or used in any manner

whatsoever without the express written permission of

the publisher, except for the use of brief quotations

for book reviews.

First Edition 2020

ISBN 978-1-925422-36-8

This book is dedicated to all those who live on the land and in rural communities.

Our dreams of tomorrow are not far away,
The landscape will change in a miraculous way.
Hold on to hope and know you're not alone
You don't have to do this on your own.

I would like to thank my family and friends for believing in me.

Brett and my children you are my inspiration, my everything. Thank you for your love and support.

Mum and Dad you are both my rock and my number one fans as I will always be yours.

Glenys thank you for your honesty and endless support, for being there for me always.

*Ros, Niki, and Michael without you this book would not be here,
thank you for your support and the endless hours you have put into making my dream a reality.*

THIS I KNOW

I open the door and what do I see?
A land that is dying right before me.

The view I'm greeted with is nothing short of confronting,
The bull dust, dry dams and constant dust storms are so devastating.

Major river systems that are drying up,
It's time for the Government to wake up!

The battle of sourcing feed,
Has become a national need.

Access to fresh clean water is now carted via a shuttle,
And hand feeding stock has become a daily battle.

When times get tough and the funds get low.
We stand together and take the blow.

Our tanks may be empty but our hearts are strong,
The rains will come again it can't be too long.

Our patience is starting to wear thin,
Waiting for the sweet sound to hit the tin.

Sacrifices we never thought we would have to make,
Have now turned into our heartbreak.

Watching the skies with a glimmer of hope,
Not knowing how much longer we can cope.

Our paddocks are empty and our last dam almost dry,
But no way am I ready to say goodbye.

Until you live it, breathe it, see it firsthand,
You will never quite understand.

One day soon I will open the door,
And be greeted by green pastures once more.

The day will come again this I know,
It's just being so damn slow.

THIS IS WHAT IT'S ABOUT

Another day of searing heat,
Beating down we are nearly beat.
Unrelenting dust storms blowing down our throat,
Barren lands that can't keep us afloat.

Looking further afield to source feed,
Praying you can find a cheaper lead.
Water is scarce every drop counts,
We ration out the smallest amounts.

You hear on the news the complaints of restriction,
To use two hundred and fifty litres out here would be worth a conviction.
The drought is moving further out,
It's time the city folk learn what it's all about.

Your day starts with putting out the supplements and feed,
The chickens are watching and waiting for their seed.
The dogs water buckets are tethered to the ground,
To prevent any spillage from your hound.

You drive over your bull dust land,
Head up the back through the sand.
One dam left to last the stock till the new year,
The thought of this brings so much fear.

The household is set up to limit water waste,
All drains exit to a designated place.
The tank only has a foot or two,
You cart what you can to get you through.

Bath time is a few inches in the tub,
It's amazing how refreshed you are after a scrub.
The water isn't let down the drain,
You scoop it up and take over the job of the rain.

You sit on your veranda for a break,
And look at a scene of absolute heartache.
The only greenness left on your land,
Are the gum tress holding on in the sand.

ANOTHER DAY

Wiping the sweat from your brow,
As you step away from the plough.
Your hopes for the day are blown away,
It seems this drought is here to stay.

You look over the paddock in front of you,
In your eyes you remember a different view.
Paddocks full of grass so high,
A mixture of buffalo, couch and rye.

The gully had water running through,
Feeding the dams so they could renew.
Veggies grew in the backyard,
When life wasn't so hard.

You look over your land with a sigh,
Everywhere you look is so very dry.
Dams that have been empty for months on end,
It's heartbreaking to comprehend.

As you drive back up to the homestead,
You're exhausted and ready for bed.
But your day isn't done yet,
It never seems to end don't forget.

Horses need their supplement and hay,
This is done twice a day.
Chickens to round up and chase into the pen,
And there is always that one wayward hen.

Dogs water to top up and feed to put out,
While they run around and yap about.
The pigs need their scraps and grain,
How they would love a wallow from some rain.

Now you slowly walk towards the door,
And silently pray for it to be like before.
Your family is there with smiles and a game to play,
And you realise tomorrow is another day.

IT'LL BE OK MATE

The Darling Downs such vibrant and fertile lands,
Why have you turned to dust and sands?
The forecast is so bleak,
No more water running through the creek.

The Condamine has turned to a puddle,
Farming is a constant battle.
Water is life,
We are in some strife.
The drought has sure hit hard,
It's now in everyone's backyard.

Our eyes are watching the skies,
And forecasters are accused of telling lies.
The storms seem to go around,
Not dropping a spot on the ground.
Another year can we last?
I'm sure we can if we look at the past.

Our Plains have taken a brutal blow,
But with some rainfall life will flow.
Hold on hope and know you're not alone,
For soon our paddocks will be overgrown.
The rains will come to our parched land,
Then our gullies and rivers will expand.

The country spirit runs strong in our blood,
Now we just wait for that lifesaving flood.
The clouds to gather and the rain to fall,
This is what will save us all.
We stand together we all unite,
It'll be ok mate, It will be alright.

LOVE OF OUR COUNTRY

My heart is breaking every day,
Watching the storms go the other way.
I wake each day with the hope of something new,
Our time surely has to be due.

The relentless drought is hitting hard,
Mother Nature has dealt us a cruel card.
Hot winds blowing from the west,
And now we're getting swarmed by a tiny brown pest.

We have dropped our usage to under forty litres a day,
And we are constantly sourcing hay.
A life on the land is not for all,
It's a daily struggle that can become your downfall.

Our kids are bred tough from the start,
The love of our country is deep in their heart.
They witness an element of life,
That keeps them busy and out of strife.

A classroom is designed for them to learn,
But a day on the farm has experiences at every turn.
It's amazing how a toy truck on a dusty hill,
Can create an image that brings them a thrill.

The lights of the city have us in awe,
But we can't handle the constant roar.
Our country lands are dry and rough,
But it's peaceful and that's enough.

CLOUDS ON THE HORIZON

Storm clouds rolling in every week,
This is just a small peak.
The rains will come soon indeed,
And start growing the seed.

Oh how beautiful the grey skies will be,
The children yelling out with glee.
Slipping and sliding over the back track.
Bogged to the belly in the old Mack.

Seeing the first green shoots push through,
What a beautiful view.
A silent tear slides down your cheek,
It's over now you can finally speak.

No one will actually know,
How hard you struggled you never let it show.
The days you didn't want to look out the door,
And sat and cried on the kitchen floor.

But you dried your tears,
And held in your fears.
You put on a brave face,
And held your family together in a tight embrace.

This drought has caused devastation,
But taught you so much about preparation.
Slow the flow and adjust your technique,
Save the water that's trickled into the creek.

Soon the paddocks will be full of feed,
Your livestock will have what they need.
Tread slowly though and don't forget,
There's hope over the horizon for us yet.

TOMORROW

The plains have taken on a different view,
The clouds are playing a game of peekaboo.
So many are going bust,
Our house yard has turned to dust.

Today the skies are blue and clear,
But yesterday it had brought fear.
The only thing that is helping us out,
Is the support of our communities that's without a doubt.

Not a blade of grass to be seen,
The treetops are the only thing green.
The old gum trees are drying out,
Dropping their branches as you look about.

The dam for six months now has been dry,
When you look at the rainfall chart you understand why.
A few horses left on your block,
And for a hundred acres that's fully stocked.

The dogs are dusty and looking rather rough,
But water is too scarce to give them a bath.
The chooks scratch around the block,
But there isn't even a worm for the flock.

The children's play area is dust and dirt,
They are so resilient they don't show the hurt.
What I would give for them to have soft lawn,
To run and play on from the dawn.

To have the tanks overflow,
Would be a better tomorrow.
Water flowing down the track,
To fill up the dam down the back.

Black clouds coming back into view,
Would be a major breakthrough.
The pitter patter on the rooftops,
Will be music to your ears hearing the heavy rain drops.

Fields of green filled with yellow flowers in bloom,
Opening buds releasing their sweet perfume.
Bees buzzing and butterflies starting to flutter,
The landscape changing, taking on a breathtaking colour.

Our dreams of tomorrow are not far away,
The landscape will change in a miraculous way.
Hold on to hope and know you're not alone,
You don't have to do this on your own.

WALK WITH ME

Follow me out the door,
Come a little further I will show you some more.
I will show you around this desert you see,
That means so very much to me.

There once stood great red gums in this line,
And this bull dust here was a lush paddock of mine.
Standing tall and full of life,
As you can see we are in some massive strife.

The arid hole over the back,
That you see is starting to crack.
Is our dam that dried out a year ago,
It really was a very hard blow.

Come a little further down this track,
You will see how much is under attack.
The meat ants are the only thing thriving on our land,
You see their tracks all through the sand.

Walk with me up this way,
Listen to what the children have to say.
Hear the excitement in their voice,
This is why I continue to make this choice.

AUSSIE SPIRIT

Our love for this country is so very high,
Even though right now it's so heartbreakingly dry.
The wide open plains that show a spectacular view,
From Port Arthur to Cape Leveque.

Spectacular beaches with white satin sands,
Waves overlapping like the stroke of gentle hands.
Mountain views that leave you speechless,
As you appreciate our country's uniqueness.

The Aussie spirit is deep in our heart,
And due to this we shall never fall apart.
Mate helping mate is the motto we live by,
And nobody questions this or asks us why.

When a national crisis comes to heed,
Each and every one jumps in to assist those in need.
A nation of truly amazing support,
Offering help and aid to every port.

A land of never ending opportunity,
With so much support from your community.
Times have tested us in the past,
But the love for this country is enough to make us last.

Through the dusty fields and our dried up river,
Our pride is enough to make you quiver.
This is our land and the beauty of it shines through,
The magic of the bush is in me, and it also lives in you.

AWAITING

We are a sunburnt country
That's for sure,
Our lands are opening up,
And awaiting a great downpour.

The rains have been long awaited,
The drought has hit us hard.
Our soil moisture has now dissipated,
And turned into a bull dust yard.

Fires are ravaging across our great land,
All our emergency services are out lending a hand.
Devastation and destruction beyond belief,
Come on rains give us some relief.

Our people have banded together,
To help a nation in need.
Our government however,
Only care for their own greed.

This has become a national disaster,
A crisis beyond their repair.
The pollies can't turn their backs faster,
And so many are now aware.

Our people are standing by us all,
And fighting for our right.
Each and every one of them can stand tall,
Because they have the guts to fight.

Without water there can't be life,
Without a farmer there is no food.
We are in a lot of strife,
And no longer will be subdued.

This is our future we are fighting for,
Our hopes, dreams and so much more.
We are tough it's bred in our blood,
But we are all praying for rain and
hopefully not a flood.

AUSTRALIA DAY IN THE BUSH

Kicking dust up the back track,
Towing the kids behind the old Mack.
Your faithful Kelpie at your side,
While the kids surf the dust tide.

Celebrating Australia Day in the bush,
Now I'm dry bogged the kids have to push.
The wife's coming with an angry face,
The kids better pick up the pace.

The flies are buzzing around the crate,
And it looks like Ozzie just ate the steak.
She's gaining on us ready to give me a clout,
Oh thank god the kids just got me out.

Now we are broadsiding around the bends,
I'm in luck here come my friends.
It's time to fire up the BBQ,
And get this party started on cue.

Jumping in the dam for a quick dip,
Crikey a yabbie just gave me a good nip.
The drinks are flowing and the atmosphere has cleared,
The wife is smiling and not angry like I feared.

The kids have pulled out the old boogey board,
And Paul's trying to attach the little outboard.
Now he is skiing across the dam,
I wonder if he can afford his rehabilitation program.

Celebrating Australia Day in the bush,
Is an experience you really should ambush.
A day of fair dinkum Aussie fun,
Of pride to be an Australian for everyone.

THE RAINS ARE GETTING NEAR

The skies may be clear,
Not our turn yet here.
Our tanks and dams are dry,
Every now and then I will let out a sigh,
But positive I will remain,
That very soon it will rain.

Raindrops that give you shivers,
From the amount it delivers.
What a wonderful sight,
The image of pure delight.

The storms rolling in,
Will give us a grin.
The children playing in puddles,
That have washed away our troubles.

Lambs chasing their tails,
No more cattle hovering over bales.
Horses galloping in joy,
And farmhands to employ.

Our rivers will come alive,
The sweet water will soon arrive.
The plains will flood, the gullies will flow,
Then our paddocks will surely grow.

Yes our skies may be clear,
But the rains are getting near.
Positivity is our friend,
Till the very end.

OUR BURNING LAND

The old gums cracking and falling,
The sound in the air of their last calling.
Golden blazes licking at the treetops,
Fear and wondering when this will stop.

Our land has burnt to a crisp,
Enduring the harsh droughts now we have this.
There is only so much you can take,
Before you start to crumble and shake.

You go over your plan of escape,
And realise it's a little pear shape.
See the driveway is lined with bull oak,
Right beside you are acres of scrub owned by the neighbouring folk.

The dams are dry and the tanks are empty,
There's no water around to protect your property.
The smoke has settled down to the ground,
You're breathing it in, it's all around.

It's coming inside and choking you out,
Night time is falling and now you are starting to doubt.
The closest fire on the app,
Is starting to close in you can smell the sap.

The night will be long as you stay on alert,
Praying everyone stays safe and nobody gets hurt.
Your eyes will stay peeled to the fire maps,
In between the briefest of naps.

You go outside in the morning,
The view that hits you is so daunting.
It's a tinderbox out there,
Fires are popping up everywhere.

Our emergency services are facing a relentless battle,
The conditions out there are so hard to tackle.
To protect and serve is their highest priority,
To stand at the frontline and save our protected forestry.

THE GLOVE

The sparkle in old Trevor's eye,
Has turned to sorrow and I'm about to tell you why.
He battled on through the drought and the dust,
With the hope the rain would come and save him from going bust.

Summer has come without any rain,
It's been a long time since his paddocks have produced any grain.
The topsoil has travelled over the seas,
In a torrent of dust storms that has brought him to his knees.

He toiled from daylight till after dark,
This was no walk in the park.
Mending fences and dropping out feed,
Tending to calves as the heifers couldn't give them what they need.
For five years this has been his struggle,
Of what to keep and what to juggle.

A labour of choice, but a labour of love,
It's rarely heard of for a farmer to hang up his glove.
Upon seeing the fire coming towards his stock,
He started an endless battle that went around the clock.
Droughts and dust storms are pretty tough on a bloke,
But now he stands defeated watching his life go up in smoke.

As the embers and smoke begin to clear,
Across the field a lone heifer starts to appear.
As his view comes into focus some more,
The devastation hits him right to the core.

Years of labour taken away in a quick blow,
No way to prepare, no way to know.
A disaster of catastrophic proportions,
That could have been different if they had listened to cautions.

He looks over his shoulder and glances towards the homestead,
Thankful it's still standing there alongside his shed.
The day has been long and the years have been hard,
Now it's broke him a little more and left his land charred.

He goes and grabs the rifle and fires a shot,
The barrel goes off with the bullet flying hot.
That poor heifer won't suffer any more,
She was the last of all he stood for.

He walks to the house with his head hung low,
See this was the final blow.
As he walks up the stairs he hangs his glove on the hook,
Glances back over with one last look.

REMARKABLE HERO

Throughout the embers and the ash,
A story unfolds of little Dash.
See Dash is a Welsh pony,
He is owned by a boy called Tony.

As the fires were closing in,
Dash could feel the danger in his skin.
He scaled the barrier like a boss,
Pushed down the fence so the others could cross.

He whinnied and let them out,
Told them which way to go with a snort and a shout.
He then opened the latch on the lamb's pen,
And neighed for the dogs to chase behind them.

As the smoke flowed into the air,
Dash galloped up to the house so Tony was aware.
On this Saturday afternoon we won't forget,
Dash a pony who was much more than a pet.
Tony's family had time to prepare,
Time to gather and get out of there.

As the sky took on a orange glow,
You could see Dash leading with a bright halo.
Throughout all the sadness and the distress,
Comes a story that will surely impress.
Of a pony with a heart of pure gold,
With a tale that amazes all who are told.

FROM THE EMBERS

A charred paw reaches out,
Between the scorched ashes that are lying about.
A fluffy ear ruffles to the surface,
The little baby knows he is here to serve a purpose.

He runs in and gently lifts this sweet marsupial up,
Standing right beside him is his loyal pup.
She has managed to sniff out six so far,
Now he is running out of room in his car.

His stomach is in his throat,
As he bundles another in his coat.
The time is ticking and running out,
So he calls for more scouts to look about.

The rescue centre is ready for him to arrive,
They are ready to make sure these babies survive.
Our nation has been busy sewing away,
Making mittens and offering up their day.

So many lives have been lost,
Our ecosystem has been hit with a staggering cost.
Now our mission is to care and protect,
And save these beautiful koalas,
They deserve our utmost respect.

Photo courtesy of Nikki Hughes (NM Photography)

DO YOU REMEMBER

Another day of watching the dust storms go past,
I don't know how much longer we can last.
Trying to keep a smile on my face,
As the dust is blowing all over the place.

I once thought we were living the dream,
But now it's become a nightmare it's so extreme.
Dried up dams and empty tanks,
Mother nature is sure pulling some pranks.

Rationing out the water we buy to share,
Between us and the animals is getting unfair.
The price of feed is getting out of hand,
But as we know nothing eats sand.

The people on the land are doing it hard,
They're being dealt a cruel card.
The government is living in make believe,
We have nowhere to go we cannot leave.

Our communities are all suffering in this plight,
Trying to stand strong and put up a fight.
Water security is our biggest worry,
But the pollies don't seem to be in a hurry.

When we look over our acreage of dust and trees,
I start to wonder who can hear my pleas.
Eleven months since a decent drop,
There is no way we can grow a crop.

Now the skies have taken on a different glow,
It's like the hell gates have opened up from down below.
Fires are now raging everywhere,
So many didn't have time to prepare.

Our country is in mourning,
Our lands are now ravaged and burning.
Heartbreak and despair,
The pain and suffering is so unfair.

Our emergency services have gone above and beyond,
They have brought to the frontline a united bond.
Risking their lives at every turn,
Trying to stop this massive burn.

Tomorrow is another day,
A day I won't throw away.
One day closer, one day nearer.
For the heavens to extinguish the last ember,
And rain again like it used to, do you remember?

A CHANGE IS COMING

The ants are coming in droves,
A trail leading up the alcoves.
The little brown frog lets out a croak,
He is calling out for a massive soak.
A desert cactus in full bloom.

A change is coming very soon.
The signs are there if you look around,
Pay attention do you hear that sound?
Your country is screaming out in pain,
It's calling the heavens to release the rain.

You know the story and how it will go,
Drought, fire and then floods are the next to show.
The land has set like concrete in the harsh sun,
When the storms come the water will surely run.

But with time and a steady flow,
Fields of green will slowly grow.
Stop and listen, don't despair,
A change is coming, it's in the air.

LIQUID GOLD

Storm clouds brewing and starting to turn,
Here comes the rain we desperately yearn.
A crack of thunder pierces the darkened sky,
As the rain starts to fall it's enough to make you cry.

Tears of happiness flows down your face,
As finally the heavens show their grace.
Water is starting to run along the table drain,
With rain drops running down the window pane.

The dam is filling right before your eyes,
You watch and wait to see how high it can rise.
The frogs are letting out a symphony of croaks,
As the ground finally gets the biggest of soaks.

This is the moment you have been waiting for,
The heavens have finally released a massive downpour.
Liquid gold is flowing across the ground,
Out here there is no sweeter sound.

Now you have a chance to breath and take it all in,
For so long you have taken it all on the chin.
But now today brings hope and opens the door,
Too many endless possibilities for so much more.

HOPE

To look up at the sky with hope,
Is our only way to cope.
Some grey clouds are starting to form,
Could this be the beginning of a storm?

The other day some moisture came down,
But it was in a dust storm so everything turned brown.
The kookaburras are laughing up high in the tree,
They are also waiting just like me.

The wind is starting to whisper through the gum leaves,
Has mother nature finally heard our pleas?
To hear the pitter patter of failing rain,
Would take away so much pain.

Waking up to that wonderful sound,
Of rain hitting the drought ridden ground.
Seeing water running towards the dried river ways,
Will give us hope of some better days.

Witnessing life flowing back into our beautiful land,
Washing away the dust and the sand.
Reviving the dry barren soil,
So we can once again plant and toil.

Just as I had lost hope for the day,
The thunder erupts a storm is coming our way.
The dark clouds are rotating and putting on a show,
Then the rain starts falling all systems are go.

An amazing sight is happening right before my eyes,
Our dry dam is finally on the rise.
The leaves on the gum trees are glistening in the rain,
Washing away so much built up pain.

As the night falls the rain is coming in a steady flow,
Now I know there is hope for our paddocks to grow.
We go to bed listening to that wonderful sound,
That's bringing life back into the drought ridden ground.

TURN OF THE TIDE

For the times we have struggled,
And hung our heads in despair.

The bills we have juggled,
As we sat and pulled at our hair.

The tide is finally turning,
With a change in the air.

Our country is no longer burning,
Green is starting to pop up everywhere.

As the days go on,
The storms build further out.

It's a beautiful phenomenon,
Seeing rain after such a long drought.

The drought though is far from being over,
But has stalled that pending foreclosure.

There is a different atmosphere in the community,
Because with rain it brings new opportunity.

Forests rejuvenating and wildlife starting to return,
This experience has taught many
that they had so much to learn.

We are a nation that has banded together,
Because we realise we cannot rely on just the weather.

So standing strong side by side,
We will support each other through this unpredictable ride.

From the tip of our coastline to the fiery desert grounds,
We will work together in leaps and bounds.

RISE

The rains have come and given us hope,
But so many are still struggling to cope.
While some have now rejoiced and celebrated,
Remember so much land still needs to be rejuvenated.

Water is running across parts of our great land,
As fires are extinguished, dust storms throw up the sand.
We are a country that shifts and reshapes,
From the fertile black soil to the desert landscapes.

Crystal blue beaches to empty creeks,
Thriving rainforests to burnt out peaks.
Tranquil hideaways along that dirt track,
To the stunning sunsets in the outback.

And once this land gets into our blood,
We stand together through drought, fire and flood.
It's our love for this country that puts us through the rounds,
Then it repays us tenfold with its sights and sounds.

We will pray and continue to hope for rain,
To come down and extinguish so much built up pain.
To settle the dust and transform our great land,
But in the meantime we will lend a helping hand.

A time of hope and a rainbow stretching across the sky,
As the storm clouds start to brew nearby.
Waiting for the raindrops to fall on the desert sand,
And start to spread out across our great land.

A resilience that is straight from our core,
With a determination to give so much more.
Knowing the light is now not far away,
To come along and brighten our darkest day.

We can now rise from this reprieve,
Start to count our loses as we grieve.
We will always have determination on our side,
As we know that farm life is a rugged ride.

NATURE'S HYMN

Little green shoots pushing through,
Are becoming my new view.
A landscape that has changed in a few days,
While we watch life bloom under the humid rays.

The mares have a spark in their eye,
As another storm brews in the sky.
Water is flowing through the gully ways,
It reminds me of the good old days.

The red gums have a lustre to their leaves,
As the light catches them in the breeze.
So much beauty is shining through,
As our land starts to renew.

Children jumping in puddles with joy,
Adults joining in, there's no time to be coy.
Rejoicing in this beautiful sight,
Has become a great delight.

A once barren dam now full to the brim,
With an orchestra of frogs singing nature's hymn.
A rustle of insects erupts into the night air,
As they seek and explore everywhere.

Tears of happiness are flowing,
As our paddocks are slowly growing.
Life is coming back into our land,
We are witnessing it firsthand.

UPLIFTING

I sit here and admire a different view,
Of green grass with a sky so blue.
A month ago was a different tale,
Of raging fires and dust storms blowing up a gale.

Tadpoles hatching by the dam,
And more than enough feed for the lambs.
Flies in the millions they are so thick,
I can't forget the mozzies their bite sure has a kick.

But even though the insects are a pain,
We have been blessed with a glorious change from this rain.
Grass so vibrant and as high as your knee,
Horses frolicking with a spirit like a brumby running free.

The hope of a future that has many possibilities,
It's a new chance for us to show our abilities.
Sustainability is the key,
And to make this happen it starts with you and me.

Tammy Harrison - meet the author.

From sandstorms to firestorms and rainstorms, life in rural Australia is tough. The people who live and work on the land are a special resilient bunch.

By day, **Tammy Harrison** is a mum to four children living on the family's 100 acre grazing property outside drought-stricken Cecil Plains in Queensland.

Tammy spends her days caring for her family, sharing the farm duties, feeding the cattle, and caring for their menagerie of chickens, horses, dogs, cats, and birds.

But in the quiet of the evening, after the chores are finally finished, and her world is still, Tammy settles on her verandah to reflect on her day. Taking in the smells, sights and sounds, she has found a way to express her emotions through writing poetry.

"Writing my poems gives me a way to deal with the stress, heartbreak and also the joy I am feeling and so many others are experiencing. There are so many overwhelming daily struggles of living in the country whether it be drought, fire or flood, but we also need to remember there is also hope. By releasing my thoughts in my poetry, I want to remind not only myself, but all those who are struggling to know they are not alone."

Tammy started sharing her poetry and photographs on social media, and it struck a chord with so many, who convinced her to share with a wider audience.

Despite all the difficulties, heartbreak and despair, Tammy's love for her country and optimistic spirit shine through in her poetry, giving a great insight into the struggles and also the satisfaction of farming life.

www.ingramcontent.com/pod-product-compliance
Lightning Source LLC
Chambersburg PA
CBHW040422120526
44588CB00041B/67